WRITING IS NOT WORK

On Finding Your Voice
With Creative Writing

D. Anthony Brown

Hermit Muse Publishing

Copyright Information

Writing Is Not Work:
On Finding Your Voice With Creative Writing

Trade Paperback Edition

Contents

Introduction

When I sit down to write a new story, I aim to entertain myself first. If I can manage that, no matter how dreadful I think the tale in hindsight, I consider the project a success. Even those rare times when I re-read the story after I've finished it and sent it off to market, I only think about what I was feeling *while writing*.

If I had fun while writing, the story works for me.

What do I mean? Why do I think having fun is important? I hope to explain the answers to those questions throughout this book. For now, I'll give the short answer:

I think having fun at writing is one of the keys to good storytelling and to having a long term career as a writer.

Look at it this way... When I write, I get to sit alone in a room (I'm an introvert) and make things up (use my imagination to have adventures). How could that be drudgery?

Oh no! Don't make me sit in that chair and be lazy for a few minutes! Don't force me to make-believe!

Yeah. Approaching fiction writing like it's "work", or something to be "struggled with", is just flat silly.

Writing is not work.

But so many people, professional writers included, approach writing as work. You hear this all time.

I churned that one out.

I toiled on this book for five years.

etc.

Serving tables in a busy restaurant is work. So is cleaning hotel rooms. Or lugging 500 pounds of high heeled women's boots on a pallet jack. (I exaggerate the weight only slightly.)

Fiction writing is just pure joy. But you have to get the right attitude first, which means clearing out some of the old clutter in your brain. You're not churning, toiling, slaving, or any work related word.

You're sitting alone in a room and making stuff up. Have a blast. Go on adventures. Enjoy the ride.

I hope this book helps you find that spot where you're having fun while writing, whether during National Novel Writing Month (commonly abbreviated as NaNo) or any other time of the year.

A Slice of My History with NaNo

In 2008, right as the Great Recession was first turning ugly, I had a career that ended before it really started. I managed to find full-time work, but not in a job that had anything to do with what I had just spent the last year studying. I was at a cross-roads, and in need of something with more of a future. I decided I didn't enjoy the career I had just trained for, but I had few other marketable skills.

But I could write.

So I researched fiction writing. What does it take to get published and paid? What do I need to learn? What am I lacking?

During this research, I stumbled across National Novel Writing Month—a yearly challenge in November to write 50,000 words in one month. I accepted the challenge, and wrote 44,000 words of an unfinished sword-and-sorcery novel. That story, which will forever remain in the trunk, was the beginning of the Brin Callahan/Tales from the Square science fiction universe, which I still write in.

From 2008 to 2014, I've completed three 50,000 word novels during NaNo. *Enchantment* in 2009 (retelling of Midsummer Night's Dream, set in Scandinavia, with trolls). *Six Dead Orchids*, in 2010 I think (spirits of children trapped in houseplants, if I remember correctly). And *Vox Banjo*, in 2011 or 2012 (early stab at my Vicki Meyers character... a Chandleresque detective with psychic powers).

Along the way in Nano-land, I also wrote a 30,000 word short untitled romance novel, where all the action took place over the telephone. I admit to being a wee bit proud of that one, since to this day I can still tell which character is saying what, even without tags. I've thought of re-opening this project and adding in setting, something I apparently didn't know how to do then. Alas, this novel still sleeps on my hard drive.

I've also been known to write short stories in November, because I have the attention span of a live-wire puppy. I believe *Bloody Rose's Echo*, an early short story featuring my Mortimer Leblanc character, was written during NaNo. I say this, because I remember a certain short-haired blond (not saying names) poking fun at the character's name. Many of the other short stories are forgettable. Many featured trolls or D&D style settings. *The Peanut Thieves*, a little thousand word short, sticks out in my mind as a fun story to write.

For Nano 2014, I explored and created my Rabid Squirrels Guild universe—a science fiction world with gamers in virtual reality. That novel—*Nerdrage the Barbarian*—did not get completed that year. In fact, at this point I'm considering tossing the manuscript and redrafting with a clean slate.

But one of the subplots to that book took on its own twist. It was a silly side adventure with two characters named Ormusen and Kalati, but this subplot was the bit I looked forward to writing the most. In December, looking back over what I had written, I discovered the subplot became a story unto itself. I cut it out from the novel and turned it into a short story titled *On Rabbits, Holes, & Shivs*. Later, I re-discovered another loose subplot in that book, and turned it into another short story called *The Devs Must Be Crazy*.

Here in late June 2015, I have no idea what I'll write for NaNo this year. Not one clue. I'm too busy writing *The Lydia Ludwig Affair* (a Brin Callahan novel) to think that far in advance.

I do know I'll be a Municipal Liaison (ML) for my home region again, for the second year. The ML for NaNo is something like community organizer, representative, and forum moderator all rolled into one. I fill the calendar with events, answer folks' questions, report trolls (thankfully I don't have any in my quiet little region, *knock on wood*), and encourage the locals to write novels for at least one month. Great fun.

What Does It Mean to Find Your Voice?

Fun fact: when you talk, your skull vibrates slightly. Your inner ear also vibrates—ear drum, stirrup, cochlea, etc.—and this changes the way you perceive your own voice. This is why, when you record yourself, your voice sounds different than what you expect. It's not because the recording machine is "cheap" or "defective"... it's recording exactly what you sound like.

But you're inside your own head. You have little basis for knowing what you sound like.

A similar phenomenon happens with writers. To my eyes, my writing is dull. Which is why, as a general rule, I don't read my own stories. I already know what happened. I know how it happened, too. Also, I live with my own thoughts 24/7, with no way to escape. My writing is simply my thoughts put into little black code on paper, and none of it feels fresh or original to me.

But the stories that I think stink too badly to be published, those same tales are the ones my first readers enjoy the most. Why is this? Because they were written with my own unique voice, in the way only I can tell a story.

I don't see my originality in front of me, because it came out of my head. I'm aware of my own tics and favorite phrases. I tend to gravitate towards certain types of characters and settings, and I'm also aware of those biases. Once written down, the story becomes dull to my attention-deficit brain.

With enough practice, though, I've learned to trust the voice I can't hear properly. I'm still practicing and

learning, with every new yarn. This is all about attitude: no more "I gotta work on my novel". I simply
trust that when I'm having fun, I'm always now subconsciously writing the story with my own voice.

I find characters and stories that excite me, and
that's what I write. I look forward to writing everyday,
even on the days when I'm avoiding my writing.

Yes, have a work ethic. Meaning, find ways to get
to the chair and stay in the chair. Work harder than
everybody else.

Just don't call writing work. Instead make it fun.
When writing is fun, you'll discover your voice.

The theme of this little book is finding your voice.
How do you develop it? Where does it come from?
How do you know when you've found it? I'll try my
best to stab those questions and provide techniques
of getting out of your own way and finding your voice.

Unfortunately, voice can't be taught. You have to
find your voice for yourself. I hope what I share here
will help.

Chapter One
Walk Your Own Path

Whenever somebody, no matter who, gives you writing advice, make sure your BS detector is turned on. No matter how friendly, well intentioned, or seemingly informed the person is. This includes me and any advice I give in this book or my blog. I'm a neo-pro—a new professional—so everything I say should be taken with a grain of salt. Take what works, leave the rest.

A few reasons for this. One, in our modern electronic age it's way too easy for anybody to create a blog or publish a book. Lots of noise out there, not all of it is good or even knowledgeable advice. And not all of it applies to you and your circumstances.

Which leads to the second reason: Every writer is different.

Let me repeat that in bold face: **Every writer is different.**

This is an important concept that I'll be returning to frequently in this book. My chosen methods don't work for many people. I won't even be discussing my methods in any great detail, partially because I doubt most of you reading this will care to learn my dirty tricks. Also, in depth discussions about writing without an outline and dealing with writer's block are outside the scope of this book.

What I hope to do is help you find your voice in fiction writing. Meaning, discover your own unique perspective, tone, and delivery in your writing. To find your creative voice, you must be an individual. Take into account your needs and passions, your limitations and experiences, and everything that makes you who you are.

All of this builds into your voice, which only you have.

Want to stand out from the crowd and sell stories? You'll need to bring your voice. Otherwise you're only mimicking what others have already done.

I don't mean never learn from others. Always learn, no matter the source. In art museums around the globe, you'll see novice painters and graphic arts students with sketch pads copying the paintings.

Will all those people copying Van Gogh become Van Gogh wannabes? No. They are trying to master the techniques of those who came before them. Then, when they are ready, they'll make those skills their own.

But first, what do I mean by *voice*? Let me share a personal anecdote to illustrate this concept.

A Story About Finding Voice

During the summer of 2014, I had the privilege of hiring a bestselling author to copy-edit and critique some of my work. I went into this arrangement with the attitude that I wanted to learn how to be a better writer, instead of simply working to make the stories she read better. I learned a ton from this author, and am forever grateful for the experience.

One of the stories I had her read was *The Silent Yearning of the Bijounonc*, a Brin Callahan story about 7,000 words long. The Brin series takes place in the Andromeda galaxy and features oddities like a corporate empire managed by an artificial intelligence, a tax agency operated like the Mafia, and evil unicorns that can teleport through space-time. These stories are near always tongue-in-cheek and very "soft" on the science fiction elements.

Silent Yearning was of my early attempts at writing to Lester Dent's "master plot formula" (a topic that deserves its own book). I wrote the tale quickly in the first half of 2014, only getting stuck around the one-third point, and in the editing phase I only fixed a few minor issues: clarity, typos, a Chekov's gun problem.

I thought the story was awful. I cranked that one out. I thought the plot device was silly, and ill described. The action, as I remembered it, was lame. And one of the characters rather conveniently disappears midway through, and reappears later with little to add.

That was all my **critical voice** talking. I'll discuss this concept more in later chapters. For now, just understand critical voice is the little whiny voice in your head always telling you things like: *you're not good enough, this story is crap, why bother*, etc.

I turned in the story anyway, knowing the best-selling author would tear it apart limb by limb.

She ended up loving *Silent Yearning*. Sure, she spotted things that could've been better, but overall she praised the story a lot. I know I got a fair critique from her, because another story I sent her—one I thought was technically superior—got some serious thrashing. (And, looking back, rightfully so.) The difference? This is pure subjectivity, but I think I tried too hard on that dud... to make it perfect, to make it be exciting. With *Silent Yearning*, I simply told a story, consequences be damned. And I had way more fun doing so.

I could not see my own voice in those two stories. The one I thought was better (*Cuts Both Ways*, for anyone curious) turned out to be a dud when looked at by someone with a clear, objective eye. The one I honestly thought was a dud was the better story. Again, when looked at by someone other than me.

Recognizing my own voice hasn't gotten any easier with more stories. The thing that has gotten easier (somewhat) is trusting the process. I say *somewhat*, because of critical voice and fear issues, which I'll expand on in later chapters. For now, I'll just say that when I'm having fun making up stories, I end up telling better stories. It's a process, largely subconscious, of letting out my inner two-year old to have fun and play make-believe.

"Bling," she said.

One more little bit to the anecdote about *Silent Yearning*.

The bestselling author did have quibbles with the story, including two instances where Cal Hemingr—an alien from the planet Xalcroft IV—casually used human slang. Namely: "deal with the devil", and "bling".

I could've followed her advice and scrubbed those phrases from the story. But I published *Silent Yearning* "as is", with only minor fixes and I left in the slang. Why?

15

Subconsciously, I built in a character reason for Cal to use slang. In the story, I mentioned her penny dreadful novel collection (among other odd collections), which is presumably where she picked up on human words. Admittedly, I didn't make that connection strong, and I've made it a challenge to myself in the later stories to show that characteristic more clearly.

Cal has, essentially, become "the alien who uses anachronistic slang", and I can use that as a character tag and a way to add tongue-in-cheek moments. I could also use her slang to add conflict. Perhaps she misuses a word, which causes confusion among the other characters. Or maybe she tries to explain something to another alien, uses slang, and ends up having to explain herself more clearly... but defines the slang word wrong, digging herself into a bigger problem.

I didn't plan Cal this way. Some writers use character sheets or create short biographies when designing characters. I do none of that. I just throw a person into a tricky situation and see what happens, adding in their opinions and sensory experiences as I go. Cal using slang happened organically, only later did I look back and realize what I did. And only when someone (accidentally though) pointed it out.

Editing out the slang would've dulled the character, and maybe I wouldn't still be writing stories that feature Cal. I chose to go my own way.

Which brings me back full circle to the topic of this chapter. Walk your own path.

No matter what your workshop group thinks, or your first reader's reaction to your story, or what reviewers (real or imaginary) say. Writing fiction is about making choices only you can make. You bring your own tastes, values, and phrasing to your stories. And all this happens between your ears.

So kick out everybody else from your writing space. Only you can write in your unique creative voice. Value that voice, and give it room to play.

Easy to say, very very hard to do. I'm going to give you some techniques to get to that creative voice, and to shut out the negativity and destructive fears. But ultimately, you have to find the tools that work best for you.

Above all, have fun, and don't worry about "getting it right". There is no "right way"... only your own path.

Just go play.

Chapter Two
Critical Voice

At the NaNo kick-off party in the Rochester, Minnesota region, we have a traditional activity. I attribute this tradition to one of the Municipal Liaisons who came before me, Tom Harper (a.k.a. improg on the NaNo boards). Whether he created this activity is questionable, but I'll say he did for sake of argument.

We hold the kick-off in a coffee shop most years, often at Caribou Coffee or Panera Bread. So we're in a public place, with lots of witnesses, the echo chamber of a thousand ongoing conversations in the background, and the smell of fresh coffee and bakery goods. Everyone is given a three by five notecard and a small envelope. A jumbo box of crayons is placed in the middle of the table.

The instructions for the activity are simple: draw a representation of your Inner Editor in crayon, and stuff him/her into the envelope, keeping him/her sealed there until NaNo is over. The Inner Editor, of course, is that beady-eyed little voice in our heads that tells us when something "isn't good enough" or "could've been better". All writers have this voice to a degree or another.

Unfortunately, the "Inner Editor" never truly goes away. You learn to live with him, but it's not always as simple as licking the envelope closed.

The purpose of this little ritual is to help us get out of our own way while writing our novels. To get the Inner Editor to shut up for a month while we play in our worlds and tell stories.

How do I deal with the Inner Editor? I suppose I should clear up something first: I don't call him the Inner Editor. In fact, he's not a he, not even a personification. I call that evil little voice something much more sinister... **critical voice**.

I can hear some of the local writers saying, "Woah! What? You never talk about this."

Yeah, I don't. I know. I just smile and nod, drawing squiggly marks on my notecard, and let my co-ML take the lead because she's the extrovert of the team.

But also because critical voice is a tough subject to tackle, and also ties into the subject of fear. Much of what stops writers from creating stories is related to critical voice and fear working in tandem. We all have these issues, we all fall off from our goals when the inner demons get too loud and boisterous.

Part of my goal with this book is to give you tools and methods to nip critical voice and fear in the bud. It's not possible to get rid of these problems entirely, but they can be minimized.

Critical voice is much bigger than just editing or rewriting, far more deadly, and more insidious. "Inner Editor" implies a voice that edits the words on the page, which we all do. Critical voice goes beyond that, and passes judgment on the worth and value of the story.

What do I mean?

I'm about to dance and weave around this topic, but I'm a terrible and klutzy dancer. I will step on people's toes. I apologize in advance. This same warning and apology applies to the chapter on fear.

What Does the Critical Voice Look Like?

You know you're deep in critical voice issues when you catch yourself saying things like:

"Why should I bother?"

"Nothing I write is any good."

"This will never sell."

I could go on with more negative self-talk, but you already know what I mean. Maybe you recognize these phrases in your everyday thoughts and the casual way you talk about your writing. Good! Once you recognize it, you can do something about it.

But also recognize that critical voice is more than grouchy negativity. When you internalize this negative attitude, you start seeing writing as work. If your story is never good enough, then *maybe* if you just try ever harder and harder you'll have a magnificent, polished story that everyone will love.

Herein lies a problem: **nothing is ever perfect nor can anything ever be perfect**.

If William Shakespeare had workshopped his plays, his oeuvre would be vastly different. Imagine the Bard at a workshop. All the words he invented? Stripped out and replaced with more "common" words. The weird triple ending in *Midsummer Night's Dream*? Likely one end would've been chosen, the others edited out. "And flights of angels sing thee to thy rest!" Why not just say, "What a shame he died like an idiot?"

Greater minds than mine can point out the many imperfections of Shakespeare's plays.

Nobody is immune or above criticism. Especially self-criticism.

And you, the writer, are your own worst critic. I'm my own worst critic, too. Why? Because as the writer, you already know your story and what you tried to do with it. And stories never quite live up to the original concept in our heads. So it's never perfect. The words seem dull and uninspiring.

The story will remain dull, even when you attempt to rewrite it and polish it. The tale will start looking like every damn polished rock there ever was. Call that the death spiral.

Here's a tip: If your first reader enjoys the worst rag you've ever written, leave it as is. If the first reader says the novel really took off on page twenty, slice off the first nineteen pages. Trust the reader, especially if he's **not** a fellow writer. A trusted first reader, one who is honest and willing to be blunt, is your best friend.

All because your critical voice won't let you see the novel for the words. Yes, that's a botched jab at the "forest for the trees" metaphor.

The Zen of Writing

If critical voice is so destructive to the writing process, why do we have it at all? What is it for?

The answer is two-fold.

First, we must learn critically. You're reading this book critically, deciding whether I'm a good resource for your writing or not, which lessons to take in, what to leave behind. Learning is stressful, frustrating, and tiring at times. Learning how to write is hard, because we have to use this critical voice to master the tools of fiction writing.

Remember to not making the writing hard, only the learning. This is entirely an attitude issue. See writing as fun, something to be savored and enjoyed after a day of work. Just like reading is fun, games are fun, TV is mighty fun. Make writing the same kind of fun and you'll write far more than you thought possible.

If you're still in the early stages of learning to be a writer, you might not see the fun yet. Don't worry, keep at it. Write every day if possible. Make it a habit. Learn as much as you can.

And then shut off the critical voice when you sit down to tell stories. Trust your subconscious to use all the tools you've given it. Shoot from the hip, follow your heart, or insert your favorite corny phrase about not over-trying and over-thinking.

Easier said than done. I know from personal experience.

The second reason for having a critical voice is to keep yourself out of trouble. The nagging voice in the back of your head that tells you not to write something... That's the same voice saying you shouldn't skydive, run naked in public, or stick metal objects into electrical sockets. The critical voice does an excellent job of keeping us alive and as injury free as possible.

Even in situations that really aren't dangerous. Such as sitting alone in a room and making up stories.

Right here is the point where critical voice and fear blend together. All of us have something to fear. All fears related to writing are irrational and have little basis in reality. But the critical voice does a fine job at making us feel otherwise.

One of my goals is to help you see your critical voice and fears, so you can better deal with them. You can never entirely get rid of them, you just have to live with them like bad neighbors.

I will give you some tools and pointers on how to adjust your attitude, and minimize the critical voice, so you can approach writing with fun and let loose your creative voice. But first, I need to discuss fear.

Chapter Three
Fear

Fear is the other half of the duo that so often stops writers cold. Fear's partner is critical voice, which I discussed in the previous chapter. I can't possibly cover every fear writers face in a single chapter. Maybe in an entire book. The focus of this book is to help you shift your attitude toward writing so you can have fun while making up stories.

So in this chapter I'm simply shining a light on the topic, and giving you a few quick pointers on dealing with fear. I won't cure you of fear (or critical voice for that matter). Fear never entirely goes away, it just skulks in the corner for awhile before sneaking back up on you. But you can manage it, and learn to live with it.

And if you think you have no fears... Wow, you need to check in with yourself. Sorry for being harsh, but I need to be. We ALL have fears, every last one of us. No one is immune to this.

If your defense mechanisms are blaring code red right now, I understand. The knee jerk reaction is normal. Take a deep breath. Close your eyes. Keeping breathing, in and out. When you are ready, keep reading this chapter.

Fear is paralyzing and will kill your productivity until you're producing 10 words an hour or less. It prevents you from ever getting to the writing chair and turning on your computer. Or even worse, fear will drive you to do "research" when you should be writing. All of us have been sucked into the downward spirals of YouTube and Wikipedia. You'll find it's easier to check email for the ten millionth time than it is to write a single sentence of fiction.

What are some normal fears writers have?

Lots of fears, each individual to the writer, but I want to highlight two: the fears of rejection and failure. Let's take each in turn. I'll discuss the fear itself, and the reality behind the fear.

Rejection is a part of the business of writing. Numerous anecdotes and tales abound of writers who were rejected many times before making their first professional sale. Truth is, if you want to sell copy to magazines or corporate imprints, you will have to face rejection at some point.

Indie publishing also has it's own quirky form of rejection: lack of sales. Instead of an editor rejecting your story, readers are the ones choosing not to buy your tale. Normally when you have only a handful of titles under your name, you make few sales. If you don't know what the long tail of distribution means, I highly suggest looking that up, whether you are a writer or any kind of artist.

Fear of rejection is normal, especially in the early stages of your career. We all want to be accepted, to make money with our craft, and we want it NOW. I was no exception.

The reality of rejection is this: it's not personal. If you are lucky to have a conversation with a long-term professional editor, there's a dandy you're likely to hear: Editors don't remember the authors they buy, much less the ones they reject. It's common for editors to have 1,000 or more manuscripts in their office at any one time. Nobody can recall the names on the stories that didn't make it. Often, early on, the editor likely rejected you based on only the first few sentences, because you didn't know how to keep her reading beyond that.

Same with readers in the indie market. You're just not good enough yet to hook a reader. And readers

won't remember you, because you don't have a repu-
tation yet. I have multiple books in my Kindle that I
didn't enjoy and didn't finish reading... but I have no
idea who the authors are. Heck, I might've later read
the same author's other books, and enjoyed those.
That's entirely possible.

The key to dealing with rejection is to keep writing
and keep getting better. Never stop learning your
craft, and write more stories. Eventually, you will learn
how to hook readers and editors and the money will
flow to you. But you must be patient, and willing to
learn.

Failure is more abstract than outright rejection.
How does one fail at writing a novel? This is a bit of a
catch-all fear, and encompasses a lot of things. Perhaps failure means the book sucks. Well... what does
"sucks" mean? That it's poorly written? This is entirely
subjective. I enjoy a number of books that others feel
are flat bad. So maybe failure is when the novel never
gets finished. After all, a lot of people say they want to
write a novel, but never do.

Ahh... Here's a trinket of human psychology. A
novice will often fear failure, and the fear itself en-
sures the project never is complete, thus the project
fails. If you can wrap your head around that, you'll be
on the way to working past fear of failure.

The only true failure in writing, is not writing at all.

Here's the solution to fear of failure: DARE TO BE BAD.

I'm borrowing this concept from Dean Wesley Smith, who in turn borrowed it from Nina Kiriki Hoffman, both renowned SF/F writers. What does it mean to dare to be bad? This is a mindset that understands it takes far, far more courage and fortitude to try something and fail, than to never try at all.

Not trying is the chicken shit way out. Everyone has time constraints, physical limitations, and other problems to deal with when attempting fiction writing. Deal with your problems head on. Set a schedule for your writing, and stick to it. Set goals to work toward (e.g. 500 words a day, whatever you can handle).

Repeat "dare to be bad" like a mantra. Write it out big on poster-board and tack it above your writing computer. Dare yourself to at least try, whatever the costs. The cost of never writing is much greater than the cost of having a book that sits in a trunk and never sells.

This doesn't mean "be fearless". Again, all writers have fears, including this one. Much of managing fear is attitude adjustment. See failure as a chance to learn and grow, instead of an end. Make mistakes, and own them. Keep learning every day.

Before I wrap up this chapter, here's an assignment.

Grab a notebook and pen (can be done on the computer if you insist). Answer this question: What are you afraid of?

Take your time. Be honest. Nobody has to see what you write, it is entirely for you. By writing down your fears, you strip them of power. Often, when fears are written out, they seem silly. As in, *why was I afraid of this, again?*

Keep your response somewhere you can find it later. Read it over when you feel a fear sneaking up on you. Write down more fears.

Now, make a plan of action. What are going to do to increase your writing productivity, and thus deny your fears any power over you? Perhaps you're going to write morning pages, as Julia Cameron suggests in her book *The Artist's Way*. Maybe you write a chapter per week. Hit 1,667 words per day during NaNo.

Keep track of how you do. Be honest. When you miss, record the miss. Ask yourself, *why did I miss?* Don't make up for lost time and misses, that way leads to insanity. Just climb back on and keep moving forward.

Remember above all else: dare to be bad.

I wish you the best in conquering your fears.

Chapter Four
Attitude Is Important

Now we've examined critical voice and fear, let's look at ways to beat them back. They can't be defeated. You'll never be rid of them. It's worse than a whack-a-mole game, but you can manage your critical voice and fears.

It'll take a shift in attitude.

When we're young and are first introduced to stories, books seem unbelievably large and complex. How does the author know how to foreshadow? How did this book move me emotionally?

Books, when given emotional weight, become important to the reader. Long-term writers have tricks to deepen the emotional impact. The best writers know what readers want, and deliver. Pay your dues, practice long enough, and you too will know what your audience wants, and figure out ways to keep them invested in your stories.

But that's not truly what's *important.*

Many early stage writers believe their writing is important. They'll change the world with their stories. Sweep people off their feet. Invoke religious experiences in their audience. I believed some of that myself once. Not anymore.

Your novel is not that important. Neither is mine.

Perhaps we can argue that stories save lives. Maybe. I have a short list of novels that have affected me so deeply as to change my outlook on life. The problem with that argument is that storytelling is a subjective art. One's happy place is another's poison. No two people experience the same story in quite the same way.

But are novels curing cancer? No.

Solving world poverty? Nope.

Ending war? I only wish.

What does a novel do then?

Well, it entertains. Amuses. Makes people laugh or cry or fall in love. That's a small thing, to share your voice and vision with an audience and give them a little escape for a moment, whether the audience is one person or worldwide.

When I write a novel, I seek only to entertain myself. If I can do that, my stories have a chance of entertaining others as well. But my first audience is always me, and just me. I never consider the novel important.

Novels can never be important. Down that road lies ruin.

If the novel becomes important, pretty soon it becomes work. Tedious work, that's hard and you have to suffer for it, and every word is a strain... Uh oh...

Sounds stressful, doesn't it?

Don't make the writing itself important. Make the time you carve out for writing important, but not the writing itself. The writing has to be fun, otherwise the promise of someday writing a novel remains just that.

A promise.

I'll talk some about time management and finding time in your day (we all have time, even with full time jobs and kids and...). But here I want to make clear this attitude shift you need to make. Go play and have fun in your created universe, but defend the time you devote to writing with an iron fist. Enlist your family and friends to help you defend that time, and go off on your own to play make-believe every day.

Never make the writing itself important. It's just stories, written with little black codes on the white page. Nothing more.

Attitude is important. Attitude will make or break you in many aspects of life. Keep your attitude to writing positive. Focus on having fun. Never tell people you need to "work on your novel". Say you need to write instead. But refrain from calling writing work.

When you see writing as work, the joy gets sucked out fast.

If writing is fun, you'll want to return to it often.

Chapter Five
Perfection

Now we've established the only "important" thing in writing is attitude, let's move on to another road bump that will stop writers from being creative. Perfection.

The common advice on the NaNo forums is to never look back in your manuscript. Never change or edit until you reach the end of the story, because you'll get stuck at the earlier chapters trying to make them perfect. Instead, take notes on what needs to be changed (e.g. change character's yellow shirt to blue in Chapter 7, so on). I'll return to this "common advice" later in the book. For now, understand I agree with the reasoning behind this, but disagree with the methodology.

All authors, especially so in the early years, are susceptible to the siren call of perfection. If only the story is perfect, readers will love it! And the critics will say bubbly nice things! And it will hit a bestseller list! And...

Here's a dangerous truth you won't like: **nothing is ever perfect**. No book in the history of humankind is immune to harsh criticism. Number of rewrites doesn't matter. Some would argue the more times a story is rewritten, the worse it devolves. And skill and pure talent won't make a book perfect. I idolize writers like Elizabeth Bear, China Mieville, and Jim Butcher. All of them have flawed books in their oeuvres. (And to my eyes, the flaws don't matter too much.)

Perfection is paralyzing. Try to be perfect, and you'll never accomplish another thing in life. Perfection is what keeps first drafts in trunk, forever untouched and never sent to market, and it also keeps wonderful books from being written in the first place.

I highly recommend the book *The Pursuit of Perfection* by Kristine Kathryn Rusch. It's a tiny book, not even a hundred pages, and worth its weight in gold. If you can't afford the book, find her website (easy to find with a Google search) and look under the Business Resources tab. Go to the Business Rusch Publishing Articles.

At the moment, Rusch's blog is a bit of a mess as she's redesigning her website. What you're looking for are the three articles that comprise *The Pursuit of Perfection*: "Perfection", "Careers, Critics, and Professors", and "Writers and Business".

Read those articles for free on her website. Think about them. Your eyes will be opened. Rusch is far smarter and a much better writer than yours truly; her work can speak for itself.

The point I want to make here is this: perfection is every bit as deadly as critical voice and fear.

What do we do about this problem? Like everything in this book, it's an attitude shift, and a battle that will happen between your ears.

A big danger is in peer workshops and writing groups. Always learn from those further down the road than you. Workshops and writing groups have value in camaraderie and motivation, I'm not arguing that. But unfortunately, finding long-term professionals at these gatherings is difficult. Workshop peers will have problems similar to your own, and often won't even realize it.

Attend the workshops and events, learn what you can from your fellows. Just don't take their critiques to heart. They don't have your voice or your vision, so don't let them be a part of your writing process.

Instead, find a trusted first reader. This is a friend or family member who reads *like a reader*, without the angst and confusion of an aspiring author.

In my bumbling early days of writerdom, I made friends with a woman and fellow scribe. She is a free-spirited sort, with a disposition to tarot and yoga. Her writing style is fluid and easy going, and odd. Strange occurrences are normal for her characters, and her settings are dream-like.

We agreed to exchange stories for critique. I have no memory of what I sent her, or what her response was. I do remember my response to her story.

Saying I was harsh is probably an understatement. I ripped her tale to shreds. I made many, far too many, red lines in the document. I told her how to rewrite sentences in the way *I would write them*, with no regard to her voice. I had not a damned clue what voice was in those dark days. I wanted her story to be grammatically correct with proper word choices, even at the cost of stripping away the childlike sense of wonder in her tale.

Our friendship fizzled afterwards.

I regret that to no end. Even after I've re-established contact with her, however fleeting, we are not close like we had been for a brief moment. It's enough to know she's safe and happy, but the friendship was badly tarnished with my critique.

These days, I only allow a select group of people read my drafts. They understand I don't necessarily incorporate their line edits (when their word choices and phrasing don't match what I would say) or their critique. I remind them I mainly want a thumbs up or thumbs down, and any typo or clarification fixes.

With crits... I only use critique to figure out what I need to work on with the next story. Each tale has something I'm trying to improve or learn how to do. I never rewrite based on feedback from people who live outside my head, and I tend to ignore the worst of negative responses.

Do I fix things in the second draft? Oh, of course. I make mistakes all the time. Typos, misused words, problems with clarity. I fix crap like that. But I leave the *story* "as is" more often than not, because I've learned to respect my creative voice and all the goofball things it comes up with.

My creative voice is far smarter than my critical voice. The critical voice wants things to be perfect. The creative side just wants to tell stories and have fun.

Learn to trust that voice. Listen to it, and don't squash it underneath the weight of presumed perfection.

Have fun.

Chapter Six
Read for Pleasure

If you wanted to learn how to play the blues guitar, you'd listen to blues music in all its many forms. You'd listen to legends like B. B. King and Stevie Ray Vaughn, and try to learn how they played. When you get serious, you'll branch out and listen to all the genres that have roots in blues: country, classic rock, heavy metal, most of modern pop music.

But if you don't enjoy listening to blues, why bother learning how to play it?

The same is true of fiction writing in any genre. If you don't enjoy reading mystery, why write mysteries?

Read the type of books you enjoy. But never read books to study. Study is a critical voice activity. Tearing apart and deconstructing a novel requires a logical, critical approach, no creativity required. You don't need a creative voice to analyze fiction, just a dry eye and plenty of caffeine.

Critical voice is useful for learning. And that's okay. Learning is possible when problems are solved with a discerning approach. Problems happen when the critical voice seeps into pleasurable activities, like reading. You'll never enjoy another story if you're constantly nitpicking somebody's word choices, syntax, plot structure, etc.

If you can't get pleasure from reading, how can you expect to give the pleasure of storytelling to another reader? (I see the innuendo in that sentence. Sorry, I'm leaving it that way on purpose.)

Once, not so long ago, I tried to finish reading every novel I started. Did not matter if I enjoyed it or not, or how long it took me to stumble through the pages. No more. Life is too damn short to waste on novels I can't find pleasure in.

This is not to put shame on a book I didn't finish. Quite the contrary, I don't finish a number of tales that are probably quite good and have wide audiences. Only, that wasn't the book for me at the time. I read enough to figure out if it's up my alley or not, and then read it or move on to something else.

I no longer write reviews anymore, for that matter. Like study, review is a critical voice activity. When something doesn't work, it doesn't matter why. It wasn't my type of story. Or maybe the first chapter was too slow. Or the character disgusted me. But I don't waste time analyzing books that don't hook me.

The books that keep me up until four in the morning and make me cranky from lack of sleep the next day... those I will study, because I want to know what the author did to pull me under. I want the tools she used to put me in a hypnosis like state, so that I wasn't even aware I was reading.

I set that book aside, and copy the cliffhangers, settings, and openings as if I were writing the book. Word for word. Not always the entire book, but key moments, like ends of chapters and the beginnings of scenes.

The key is, I read for pleasure first. If I can't enjoy the book with a bag of popcorn and an appropriate beverage, it's not the book for me. I'll make exceptions for non-fiction books, but even then I want a good read that is intellectual and entertaining. For fiction, I must be entertained, or the book goes back on the shelf.

I also believe you should read outside your own comfort zone. If you want to write an epic fantasy, you should of course read fantasy of all stripes. But also seek out romances, for characterization and emotional setting. Read thrillers for pacing. Find a good mystery series to get a feel for how a detective unfolds a puzzle problem. Read science fiction for the bizarre ideas. Et cetera.

I must stress again, read only for pleasure. If you don't see pleasure in reading, you won't approach books very often. When stories become pleasurable again, you'll enjoy your writing more as well.

Finding your voice involves doing things you enjoy doing, as opposed to slugging through a tedious task (like so much else in life). Reading for pleasure is the goal for yourself, as well as the audience you want to entertain with your work. To know how to please an audience, you must first be the audience.

Chapter Seven
Time & Writing Speed

What is considered writing "fast"? How about writing "slow"? Fast/slow is a false dichotomy. I know you don't believe that, but I hope to demonstrate how you too can be considered a fast writer and a slow typist at the same time.

There will be math ahead, so be warned. I promise to keep the numbers simple, don't worry.

So first, how many words per day do you need to accomplish NaNo? Divide 50,000 words by 30 days, round up, and you'll get 1,667 words per day. What does this mean? How long does it take to produce that?

I'll make this personal—just like much of this book—and tell you my number: two hours a day. Not necessarily two hours in one massive block. In fact, I have a hard time doing that. My attention span is too short, and I'm too fidgety to sit still that long. Usually I write in shorter blocks... fifteen minutes here, half hour there, an hour before I go to bed.

Let me back up a moment, and note that I can type about forty or so words per minutes and maintain some degree of accuracy. If I typed at that rate, I could theoretically write 2,400 words per hour. But I don't.

My wrists would hurt like crazy and I'd probably make excuses to not return to the keyboard pretty soon. And I flat just don't need to type that fast. No reason to injure myself. And I can't think that quickly. My brain doesn't allow me.

Here's a secret: Most writers don't write as fast as they can type. The brain can't come up with a story fast enough to match the finger movements. We're used to telling stories as fast as we can talk. I certainly can't say 2,400 words per hour. I'd die, maybe figuratively if not literally.

I tend to average a typing speed of 1,000 words per hour, ranging from 700 to a blazing speed of 1,400, depending on where I'm at in the story. Beginnings are a bit slower for me as I figure out who the character is, what the setting looks like, etc. When I see where I'm going, I can create faster.

But I figure 1,000 words per hour (or 250 words per fifteen minute block), and I've recorded this pace enough times to know for fact that's what I do. I also know from experience I spend a lot of time leaning back in the chair, thumb under chin, eyes scrunched up as I figure out what the next sentence is.

So I'm typing less than 20 words per minute on average, when I'm being creative, and much of the creativity is happening between my ears instead of on the page.

At that rate, on average, I can complete my Nano goal in about two hours. Just a steady rhythm of output, like a drum beat. Or like a normal walking speed. I'm not sprinting or even jogging. Meandering to my goal, more like it.

This glacial speed allows my voice to come through. I give myself time to think about what comes next, and allow my subconscious to work in tandem with my fingers. Any faster, and I'd be just typing random crap, which would be crap that'd ultimately get deleted later.

What Is Considered Fast?

Let's do a thought experiment.

How long does it take to write a novel? A month? A year? Five years?

If you're normal, you have a life, with all the trappings that come with it. A job, a family to care for, pets, house cleaning to do, chores to run, a commute. Not to mention entertainment... books, TV shows, movies, music, video games. Everybody has their responsibilities and vices.

What if you were so busy you could only write fifteen minutes a day? How much would you accomplish?

If you write as fast as me, you could get around 250 words in those fifteen minutes. Let's say you write seven days a week, because you don't take weekends off. And at that strenuous pace, you need a two week vacation, so you have fifty weeks in a year.

250 words x 7 days x 50 weeks = 87,500 words per year

That's a decent sized novel. In a mass market paperback, it'd be a little under 400 pages. Not bad at all.

Think of it this way: in one year, you'll have accomplished something many people only dream of doing in their lifetime, because you sat in a chair and wrote for fifteen minutes a day.

And if you wrote half an hour a day, you'd have two novels a year and many folks would consider you prolific.

So, to answer the question to our thought experiment, *how long does it take to write a novel?* As little as fifteen minutes a day, added up over time like water from a leaky faucet being collected in a bucket. You'll get a full bucket with enough persistence and patience.

Ten to fifteen minutes here, 250 words there, all adds up faster than you can believe. Now, in NaNo, the challenge is to find more than fifteen minutes a day. Maybe you have some time in the morning before heading to the day job. Good, use it, even it's only a few minutes and you only type a page. It's a start.

You can get more on your lunch break. Perhaps another fifteen minutes when you get home, before the kids get home, after dinner, somewhere. And instead of watching *Xena: Warrior Princess* reruns, you spend a full hour before bed and get a huge number of words added to your story.

By the end of the day, you'll be stunned how you got 1,667 (or more!) words with a leaky faucet drip here, drip there. I'm certain you'll have fun, and that fun will simply encourage you to get to the chair sooner and more often. When you're in the chair more, you'll be writing faster even when it looks like you're doing nothing but daydreaming while typing a sentence now and then.

Enjoy being a "fast" writer!

Chapter Eight
Smoke & Mirrors

With some oddball exceptions, books are always read from front cover to back. Beginning to end. You don't start reading in the middle of chapter ten, go back to the prologue, and then work backwards from the end.

But you can do exactly that when you write a book. Let me give you an analogy.

Ever read Kurt Vonnegut's *Slaughter-house Five*? The protagonist, Billy Pilgrim, lives unstuck in time. In one moment, he's a soldier in World War II. The next he's a child. And then he's an old man. The story bounces back and forth in Billy's life. Vonnegut, being the genius he was, weaved a non-chronological story that makes perfect sense.

When you're a writer, you want to be just like Billy Pilgrim. Be unstuck in the timeline of your story. I rarely write in order, except maybe with short stories and even then I tend to loop back and forth from the "current" spot to an earlier point.

This book, as it *now* stands, is an organized mess. Doing a quick estimate, I'm over the 5,000 word mark, but it's hard to say because all the chapters are in different files and I don't want to break my focus. (I was actually at 8,000 words.) Most of the headers say "Chapter ?", because I don't know what order I'll present the topics. My "outline" is a checklist of things I want to discuss, written on a single piece of notebook paper in my chicken-scratch handwriting.

I have a file for a chapter on critical voice, about 400 words long at the moment. My checklist includes the topic "Fear". I'll complete the chapters for both topics, and I want them early in the book, but I've skipped them for now.

Why?

Critical voice and fear are very hard topics to discuss, and I'm not sure I have all the tools to give the chapters what they need. (That sentence is an example of critical voice.) And what I have to say will be controversial and might upset people. (And that's fear right there.)

I wasted a week—which thankfully didn't stretch into maybe weeks or months—letting that critical voice and fear eat at me while both chapters went unfinished. If I had attempted this book a year ago, I'm sure it would never have gotten done.

Note, I was still writing during that "off" week. I worked on *The Lydia Ludwig Affair* until that project too stalled—I think because I've hit the third of the way point, the magical place where new ideas lose their energy. So I switched to another project, *The Devs Must Be Crazy*, which is now near completion.

I'm aware of all this because I keep a record of what I do every day in a small notepad. Books I read, games I play, places I go, how long I work, what projects I'm on, etc. I hadn't even realized until now that a whole week had gone by without working on *Writing Is Not Work*.

The point is, I wanted to gain some momentum and move forward. So I skipped those chapters for now, and wrote on the topics that aren't so hard to write. Guess what?

I've had great fun so far. I've written a chapter a day since Sunday, and it's now Thursday. I hope to get the book done before I leave on a road trip in mid-July. That gives me eight days. (And yes, I made that deadline! (Speaking of writing out of order.).)

I've chosen to manage my critical voice and fear in a positive way, and not let them drag me to a dead stop. When I return to the chapter on critical voice, I'll have a streak going, and that will motivate me to do what I have to do.

So give yourself permission to write out of order. Kill the butler before showing Chekov's gun. Once the body is cooled and your detective has had time to investigate, then go back to an earlier point and drop the sneaky foreshadowing into the right places. Afterwards, you can continue forward with the tale and let the plot thicken.

The common wisdom of NaNo is to never go back and change what you've written until you're done with the first draft. I don't dispute that advice. Remember, every writer is different. But that's not how I work. At all.

When I finish a scene, I jot down some notes on a piece of notebook paper. Something to the effect of the chapter number, the viewpoint character's name, maybe what she's wearing, and what happens.

An example from *The Lydia Ludwig Affair*: "Chap. 2, Brin, chase Gare, into wine cellar, captured."

Enough information to remind me later what happened. Sometimes, I'll have to rewrite my backwards outline when the chapters get rearranged too much, which I'll be doing soon with Lydia Ludwig. I did a massive loop into earlier parts of the story, with new viewpoint characters. The loop was possible, and painless, because of the notes I had taken. I knew where in the flow of the story to place the new view-points.

This looping, or cycling, is not editing. I'm adding new material, entirely from creative voice. Editing and rewriting are largely critical voice activities.

Some writers will take notes on what needed to happen at an earlier point in the story—such as, ADD SCENE TO SHOW GUN—and then in a second draft add the scene. Each to his own. My preference is to just add the scene, because if my creative voice is telling me to do so, I feel I should honor that. Same with changing somebody's hair color, or the type of gun they use.

And who's to argue with adding new words, re-gardless of where those words are placed? Cycling and writing out of order helps me produce a cleaner first draft. And holds me into a story longer when I know I don't have to do heavy edits to fix little things.

The end result to the reader is the same. No read-er will be able to tell the difference when a writer cy-cles or not. The act is smoke and mirrors, an illusion of continuity. It wasn't a continuous story in the writer's head, now it is in the reader's.

You just don't need to tell anyone you wrote that fun, fast paced tale out of order.

Chapter Nine
Empathy

One of the single most useful skills in a writer's toolkit is empathy. The ability to understand another person's point of view, to see things from another's eyes, to walk around in the other's shoes.

Yes, you should write what you know. But stories often demand a viewpoint that comes from outside your head. How would alien beings ever get written? How could men ever write about women? Or women about men? How can a geriatric understand a teenager?

Empathy.

This will be a short chapter, and I almost didn't include it, but I think it important to drive home a point.

In order to develop rich, thick worlds with a variety of characters, you must at some point write about people who are not you.

I'm an introvert, severely. I have to talk slow and extra loud in crowded rooms because I don't always enunciate my words clearly. I look like Seth Green's evil clone, and about the same height. I have certain bends on religion and politics, which shall remain private. I enjoy reading, playing video games, and TV crime shows. I have two life long passions: astronomy and dinosaurs.

And if all my characters were mini-me's with fake mustaches, I'd stop writing out of boredom. Not that I don't write characters who mirror me, but the common trait is usually obscure or small, if even there. I prefer to write about people who definitely aren't me, because I enjoy stories about characters who take dangerous risks I would never have the guts to do myself.

And how does this relate back to finding your voice as a writer?

Empathy allows you to do more than just write characters who are not you. Empathy also lets you into the hearts and minds of your audience. Readers don't pay attention to flat and dull stories with no emotional tug.

Ever notice something on TV crime dramas? Besides the central character and his or her sidekick, the supporting team has a certain cast. A white guy, a black guy, often someone of another ethnicity, and at least one woman. You see this pattern in *Criminal Minds*, *Numb3rs*, *Crossing Jordan*, and many other shows. Why do the creators do this?

Quite frankly, so the show appeals to as wide a base as possible. We subconsciously identify and empathize with people who are like us. Keeping a diverse cast of characters allows the show to throw a wide net and attract a bigger audience. As fascinating and tense as *Numb3rs* was, I doubt the show would have been as popular without the characters Megan and Amita.

Audience is crucial; never underestimate the whims of the folks you set out to entertain. So show the readers you don't write cardboard characters in plastic stage scenery. Breathe life into your characters and give them qualities and personalities that live beyond the page.

Practice empathy by observing other people. Watch their body language. Are they open, with shoulders back and head high? Do they glance nervously about? How do they walk? Interact with the people around them?

Write these things down in a journal. Practice making your fictional character do things besides smile and frown. Tougher than it sounds, and takes much attention to detail and practice. But one day you'll have characters with tightly pressed lips, cheeks blushed and dimpled, shooting peas from his nose as he vainly hides that not so generic smile.

And then go even further by climbing into the character's head. Remember the original *Men in Black* movie? You know the scene in the morgue where they open the jeweler's head and inside is a tiny alien.

You want to be the alien in the guy's head. Experience the world through the viewpoint character's senses: sight, sound, touch, smell, taste. This is the value of showing, right here. *Show* what it feels like to trapped in a crowded train station: shirt sticking to sweat soaked skin, strangers' bony elbows digging into your sides, endless sea of faces, the smell of too many bodies on a hot summer day.

All from the eyes, ears, and nose of the character.

Have fun at playing with viewpoints. In the next chapter, I'll dig deeper into depth of sensory detail.

Chapter Ten
Barn Words

During your adventures in Nano-land, you're likely to encounter what I call *accounting tricks.* These are ways of artificially fluffing your word count, and have nothing to do with the art of storytelling.

Some examples will help explain what I mean:

Expanding your contractions. Meaning, instead of writing *isn't,* your write *is not,* which gives you an extra word.

Give a character an extremely long title, and make him insist the other characters call him by that. For example: High Lord Exarch Captain Peter McDonald, First Class, of the Calimre Squad in New Botswani Across the Sea.

Include long, descriptive chapter titles. This is the chapter where... blah blah blah, etc. happens.

Let me be clear: none of these techniques are "cheating" at NaNo. Not too many ways to cheat at this challenge, to be honest. You can randomly generate 50,000 words of *lorem ipsum* (i.e. fake text that looks pseudo-Latin) and claim that as your "novel". That would be cheating. I'm not calling any accounting tricks cheating. You do whatever you have to do to make words appear on the page.

Also, there are times when an accounting trick can accomplish a literary function. Say, if you have a character who doesn't speak English well, you might expand his contractions to show how slow he is at talking.

But if you want to develop your voice—that raw edge that gives your fiction its own sound—I'd recommend staying away from accounting tricks. Technically you can go back and edit your contractions back down, and slice off all the references to High Lord Exarch What's-His-Name.

But editing and rewriting are different skill sets from writing. I can't prove that to you, certainly not in a short article like this. So you'll have to take my word for it.

The skill you want to develop is that white-hot heat of the moment creative voice that you only get while putting fresh words on the page. Accounting tricks often polish away that uniqueness.

But... but... but... How do I get 50,000 words in a month?

I'm going to show you a trick that will not only help you learn voice, but also flesh out your characters and settings, thicken your plot, and maybe even help you move forward when you're stuck.

Ready?

What Do You Mean? Barn Words?

Early beginning writers have a common problem. I was no exception, and still have this problem though I've gotten better. Here's the issue: beginners often use dummy, non-descriptive words to describe complex objects.

Dean Wesley Smith calls these "barn words". Meaning, words that should describe something, but don't, at least not by themselves. These are common barn words: barn, horse, tree, apple, human, hill, house, cup, etc.

We all know what a barn is? Or do we? I live in the Midwestern United States, where barns have a certain look—often red, a steep roof with a hayloft, big double doors—except when they don't look that way. And a barn in Minnesota looks very different from a barn in Vermont. Or a barn in Pakistan. Or a medieval French barn.

But descriptions don't end with sight. What does the barn smell like? Depends maybe on what it's used for. Does the barn make creaky noises during thunder storms?

Go crazy putting in **all five senses**, from the viewpoint character's perspective. When you put in sensory details, you'll develop the character far above and beyond any height/weight/eye color fill-in-the-blank descriptions you can come up with. Your novel will have words that don't feel like padding. And you'll develop your voice.

Let me give an example.

Random Story Prompt Time!

I flipped through the Webster's dictionary to a random place and stuck my thumb on a random spot on the page. The nearest noun that caught my attention was *library*. I want to begin a story with this word.

She waited at the library. (5 words.)

The scene is clear as mud, right? You know exactly what I mean by "waiting at the library". Well, no you don't. I have a certain image of libraries, created by my experience of being in many such buildings all my life. You have your own image. What I gave you in the sentence above may as well be a white room for the character to float around in.

I'll try again.

She waited at the library, hunkered down in the upper floor non-fiction section where the windows were all blown out. Only one lonely pane of glass remained, covered in handprints and dust. The sour wind whistled through, carrying the gunpowder smell of mortar to mix with the smell of yellowed paper wet with rain dripping from the broken roof.

Bombs exploded across the ruined husk of a city. Somewhere, not far away, a building collapsed. The thunderous boom rattled the library's floor under her feet.

Books lay scattered like dead soldiers on the ugly brown carpet, pages fluttering and turning in the wind. In the corner of the reading section, a pock-marked and bullet-ridden reproduction of the Venus de Milo stood guard over the "corpses", like a broken Valkyrie over a battlefield of dead knowledge.

Grimacing, teeth clenched on the leather strap from her pack, she tightened the dirty rag around the bullet wound in her thigh. Enough to stop the bleeding, and to make her double-over in pain. Not enough to dull the throb to a pins-and-needles ache. Cheap whiskey helped, even if it made her throat dry as the book on astrophysical teleportation she had her head pressed against.

She checked her AK-47. Only half a clip left. After that, she'd have to rely on the sniper rifle. She had a "Dirty Harry" style revolver on one hip, with a single bullet in the chamber. She was saving that for later.

(243 words.)

Not what you expecting, huh?

Not only did I add 238 more words, I also gave you a better sense of what I meant by "library".

This deeper sense comes not from the word choices per se, rather from the sensory details I chose to convey. I threw in sight (the window pane, the Venus), sound (explosions), smell (mortar, yellowed paper), and taste (whiskey, her dry throat). Looks like I missed touch, but perhaps my eye isn't seeing it. Four out of five senses ain't bad.

I also have a good feel for this character, who didn't exist twenty minutes ago. My impression so far: she's a Lara Croft-style heroine, hardboiled and gritty, and knows what needs to be done. And I started some neat world-building. This could be an alternate reality dystopia. Astrophysical teleportation exists alongside AK-47s.

I managed to give my heroine a serious problem. She's alone in a warzone, wounded and with diminishing resources. And there's some mystery. Who is she waiting for? Who is the bullet for? A rival? A traitor? Herself?

I have no clue what happens next. None, at all. I won't even know if this is a novel or a short story until I finish the first scene or two. Then I'll have a better sense of how this story is paced, and how complex the character's problem really is.

When I tell people I write into the dark, with no outline or plot idea in mind, this is what I mean. I often start with little more than a scene concept, or a title, or a stupid prompt like *library*. I then climb into the character's head and add as much sensory detail as I can squeeze in. Often, once I've established my character's perspective and her attitudes, I inadvertently give her a big problem to deal with.

Then I form a scene that ends with a cliffhanger or a twist, which leads into another scene. Et cetera.

You can do this, too. And fill an entire novel. I find adding all five senses at least once every 500 words works powerfully.

Just find your barn words and ask, *how does my character experience this thing, in both mind and body?*

Above all, have fun with this technique.

Chapter Eleven
Write Scenes

How do you eat an elephant?

This is a favorite question bandied about by business gurus, especially entrepreneur experts and motivational speakers. The elephant question is framed around discussions about how to tackle big projects. You know, the projects that seem insurmountable and feel like they'll take forever to accomplish.

Kind of like... you guessed it, writing a novel.

The answer to *how do you eat an elephant?* is *one bite at a time.*

Very few people can hold an entire novel in their head. In fact, I've never met somebody who could. And if I ran across such a person, I'd have unspoken doubts about their claim. Perhaps an already completed story can be contained in your head, maybe. But a novel you haven't written yet? Nope.

Just doesn't work that way.

Even if you outline the story ahead of time, you still won't be able to do so. I write into the dark (meaning, no outline), sure, but I've experimented with outlines. Every time, no matter what style outline I played with (Randy Ingermanson's snowflake method, Lazette Gifford's phase outline, nine-act movie outline, etc.), the story always turns out different from whatever I originally envisioned. (When I've completed the story I outlined, truth be told. Outlining sucks out the joy of discovery for me, so a number of stories never got finished because I already "knew" what happened.)

Read enough how-to books by long-term professionals, you'll find the common advice is to not enslave yourself to your outline, no matter how "perfect" it may seem at the time you write it. The outline is a great way to organize a novel before you write, which is why people use them.

So, in the act of eating this novel-sized elephant, if outlines help only marginally and writing into the dark (or "pantsing", for those who prefer that term) has few built-in mechanisms for organization... How do you eat the elephant?

The answer is summed up by two words: write scenes.

Pin that phrase to the top of your computer where you see it every time you sit down. Repeat it like a mantra. You're not writing a novel overnight. Write a scene instead.

Only focus on one little scene at a time. What is the character doing? Where is he (the setting)? What does he want? What's stopping him from getting what he wants? Answer questions like that for every scene. Then start another new scene.

Now for the obvious question.

What Is a Scene?

A scene is a short part of the story (500 to 1,500 words long) that features: a **character** in a **setting** with a **problem**. The character **tries** to solve the problem with his own training, skill, or brawn; and **fails**. The failure results in either a cliffhanger or a plot twist, which leads into the next scene.

Novels are a collection of these try/fail cycles. The character continuously tries something, fails, tries something else, maybe has limited success, but fails, and keeps trying/failing until the **final try** (a.k.a the climax).

A single scene can make up a chapter. Or a chapter can be several scenes stitched together, with white space in between (or no white space). No wrong way, just your own.

Note the word count range... 500 to 1,500. A quick scene can be 300 words. A long scene can go as high as 2,000 words. But the thousand word average is the sweet spot for Western readers (those in the Americas, Europe, and Australia primarily). If the scene drags for too long, you test your readers' attention span.

The chapters in this book are averaging around 1,000 words. I've written so many scenes by this point, that this length is nearly automatic. At 500 words in I have a good sense of where I'm going. When I hit around 1,000 words, I'm looking at how to wrap up. And I usually manage to do just that within another 500-so words, though occasionally I'll write past my cliffhanger. No big deal when that happens. I simply cycle backwards a bit, find the cliffhanger (and it's always there, my subconscious plants it without me knowing), and chop off the rest.

Then, new scene. Or with non-fiction like this book, new chapter.

How Do You Build Scenes?

On to the business end of scene writing. Where do we start?

At the beginning of a story, I often start with a setting. I pick a place—a house, a room, a garden, whatever—and climb into my character's head. Sometimes I don't know who my character is until I've written a few hundred words. Some characters, like Brin Callahan, have a certain "voice". I'll be typing away, poking along with the story, and around 300 words in I'll suddenly say, "Oh yeah, this is Brin talking."

I add in five senses. Taste, touch, smell, sight, sound. I show my reader the setting. Never, never intrude in authorial voice and tell your reader, "He turned his head, and saw this, that, and that." Show the reader by pulling her under surface of the words and into the story through the character's experiences.

They're not just pretty flowers in a garden. Oh no... These are dark red roses, the color of blood in the moonlight. Dead and wilted, but crisp and fragrant to an oversensitive nose. The sweet, funereal scent mixes with the coppery taste in your mouth. The gravel crunches under your weather-worn boots. A western wind blows early snow in your face, minuscule icicles pelting your skin like a million mosquitoes. But you don't feel the cold. No shiver traces a finger down your spine. Just the ancient rush of the hunt... (Just a random character I made up on the spot to show sensory detail.)

Now, let's discuss the real problem. What is your character's problem?

Problems can be anything, but they can't be easily solved. A problem could be: *I want a ham sandwich.* But nobody's around to fix it for me. So I plug in the toaster, and open the fridge, and...

Get sucked into a vortex and dropped into a desert.

Already, my mind has turned this into a Bruce Campbell character (*Evil Dead* movies, for those who don't know). Getting sucked into the vortex would be the cliffhanger of scene one. I'd cycle back and add in some mystery as well, to make it more interesting. Such as: Where is everyone? Why is Bruce alone in the house?

In scene two, Bruce has bigger problems than being hungry. Now he's lost. But there's a fortress in the distance. Maybe he can get help there. But he gets captured along the way. Who are his captors? Another cliffhanger, more mystery for Bruce to fathom.

Add in five senses every 500 words or so, to make it feel like it's all inside Bruce's head and he's the one with the eyes, ears, nose, tongue, and skin. And keep repeating the try/fail.

Until the end when Bruce saves the day, kisses the damsel, and tosses the Big Bad Guy into a catapult and sends him flying to the horizon. (Maybe even in that order.) Or whatever endpoint comes naturally to the story.

The key is to keep writing, one bite-sized scene after another.

Have fun, wherever the story takes you next.

Chapter Twelve
Project Block

I promised myself this book wouldn't be about busting writing myths. I figured all would be good if I could get people to understand critical voice, fear, and creative voice. But there's a lot of myths out there about writers and the writing process, many of which are ugly and in fact are deeply held beliefs by many people. I wanted *Writing Is Not Work* to be helpful to the beginning fiction writer.

Busting myths and breaking apart belief systems, no matter the intentions, is rarely conducive to learning in the early days. I feel it's enough to get the basics here.

However, there is one particularly deadly myth I need to bust, because everyone going through NaNo will experience this in one form or another.

Writer's block.

Before I go further, if you are having difficulty getting to the writing chair, I highly recommend *Break Writer's Block Now!* by Jerrold Mundis. It's a quick read, you can through it with all the writing assignments in an afternoon or two. And you'll learn a lot of things I'm only scratching the surface of here.

Dealing with writer's block is another attitude shift, one that everyone can accomplish. By the time you've learned this new attitude and made it your own, you'll no longer need the term writer's block. Banish the concept from your mind. Give it no power over your art.

Writer's block is a myth, plain and simple. Like the "men in black" conspiracies, writer's block has sunk so deep into popular culture nobody gets the joke anymore. If there ever was a joke. Professional writers have no need for writer's block.

Imagine having "job block". *Oh darn, I can't come in today boss, I have job block!* How would that go over? Same thing with professional writers and storytellers. When your career, your bread and butter, is writing then you have no time or energy for writer's block.

Don't Believe Me?

I understand if you don't believe me. Really, I do. Writing can be so very hard at times. Painful even.

But there's nothing wrong with your ability to write. Are you having trouble getting started on your writing? Is it writer's block?

Try this: Get out a piece of paper. Write on the top line *I woke up in the middle of the night.* Set a timer for fifteen minutes. Now write about what happened when you woke up. Doesn't matter what you write, if it's true or not, or even believable. No one is going to read this. Doesn't need to be good or bad or indifferent. Just write.

I'll wait while you do this exercise...

Done? Okay. Most people can get 200 to 300 words in fifteen minutes. Some write slower, others faster. Doesn't matter, because you wrote.

I just proved you didn't have writer's block. There's nothing wrong with your brain's ability to put words on paper. No mental defect or physiological reason for your previous difficulty with writing. No writer's block.

There are some afflictions that make writing harder. Depression, anxiety, and addiction come to mind. Mental illness is hell, and if you suffer from a psychological disease, please seek help. Get therapy.

Writer's block—the inability to write—is not a disease, and only has power if you believe in it. Easier said than done, I know. Especially when there's also *project block*.

What Is Project Block?

Something that happens to all writers at some point or another is project block. This is when a project—be it novel or short story—comes to a grinding halt. Many reasons for a project to suddenly slam the brakes, none of them have to do with the mythical writer's block. Remember that. Nothing is wrong with your ability to produce words.

But it's okay for a project to be blocked. It happens to all of us. And there's ways of beating project block, which I'll discuss. First, what are some causes of this type of block?

Commonly, writers during NaNo will get stuck around the second week. This is a time when word counts commonly are forgotten until the November 20th or so, and sadly many writers give up and drop out altogether. Why the second week?

If you're hitting the 1,667 daily words goal, around the middle or so of week two is when you're hitting the one-third area of your book. The so-called "middle" of the novel. This is a very tricky place to be when writing a novel, but not because of any craft or storytelling related issues. I can't give a satisfying reason for this, but after the first third, all novels lose their energy and freshness *for the writer*.

Again, this happens to everyone. No one is immune to the one-third spot deathtrap. So don't feel alone. The characters won't feel as special and unique, and the story starts feeling slow and dull. I'll discuss a real simple technique to get past this below.

It's also possible you're not ready to write the novel. You might be going along and happy with your progress when suddenly your subconscious says, "Nope. Not happening."

Only you can figure out if this is the case. I've had this issue with my Spare Parts universe, because the relationship between Geraldine Montess and Mortimer Leblanc grew complex... and rather personal. I've yet to finish a story with Geri and Mort working together as a team, like they should, solving necromantic crimes. Hasn't happened because for a long time I wasn't ready to write about their odd-couple relationship.

Maybe you took a wrong turn in your story. Whether you outline or write into the dark, it's always possible to head in a wrong direction. Every time this happens, your subconscious will rebel and pout like a two year old. This is tough to recognize when you're a beginner, because you don't know what you're doing wrong (or right, for that matter).

Fear can also a cause of project block. Fear of finishing a story. Of letting other people read a story. Any number of highly personal fears can sneak in and strangle a project.

Those are the top four causes: the one-third point, not ready to write on a given subject, taking a wrong turn in the story, and fear. Now, what do to do about project block?

Tricks for Getting Back to Writing

Here are some hardcore techniques for overcoming project block. I'll start with the one everybody is going to like.

Take a nap. Sleep on it. But there's a trick to this. As you fall asleep, tell yourself you'll figure out the story when you wake up. As you sleep, your subconscious will do the work for you and you'll be able to approach the novel with a fresh eye.

Write the next sentence. The key to writing a novel is to keep writing the next sentence. What happens next? Write it down. Then write another sentence. Keep doing that until you reach the end. Easier said than done. Trust your voice. Trust the subconscious. And write one more sentence. One after another.

Go back three chapters, or whenever you feel you started grinding to a halt, and delete. This will annoy the NaNo purists, but I don't care, because it works miracles to free up your mind to play. Cut the last three (or more, if necessary!) chapters of your novel and go in a different direction. Save the cut material in a trash file so you still have the "word count", but consider it no longer part of the story. Finding a fresh angle will keep the tale from feeling bland and predictable to you.

Get a prompt. Remember what I did in the chapter on barns words? Flip through a dictionary to find a random word, and make that the setting for your next scene. Or use a random story generator to give you ideas. Lots of online generators, as well as dice games and such out there.

Set a timer. Besides nap time, having a timer has probably worked the best for me productivity wise. Set the timer for fifteen minutes or half an hour (or a full hour, but I have a hard sitting still for that long). You can do nothing but write during that time. No checking email, no "research", no texting, no phone calls. Only writing. Eventually your mind will get so bored, you'll start making up stories to entertain yourself.

Once the timer is up, take a break. Come back later and set the timer again. Keep repeating until you get to your goal.

Switch projects. Here I go, angering the purists again, but darn it if this doesn't work. I'm not the typical wrimo, if you haven't noticed by this point.

Supposedly, Isaac Asimov had multiple typewriters, each set up with a different project. When he got stuck with one book, he'd move to the next typewriter and keep writing. I've never been able to confirm this story, to be honest, so I might be confusing Asimov with somebody else. But I like the image.

Asimov knew the most important thing he could do was keep writing. He was among the most prolific authors of the pulp era for a reason.

Be like Asimov! Switching projects is especially important when you're not ready to write a certain book. I'm known for writing short stories during NaNo. When I do so, I'm often stuck on my novel.

The trick here is to write something completely unrelated to your novel. if you're writing an epic fantasy, go kick off a mystery short story. Write a different genre, with new characters, a fresh setting, a very different plot problem. Give your mind a break from the project that's kicking your butt. But keep moving forward. After all, every word counts during November, whether from a novel or whatever.

Remember: writer's block can't exist for you. Give the myth no power by changing your attitude. You can have project block. But keep writing.

One more thing, a word of warning. When in a workshop, a write-in, or any gathering of beginner writers, never say aloud that writer's block is a myth.

You won't make any friends that way, and may end up making enemies. Trust me on that.

But you can subtly correct people. "No, I'm not having writer's block. My project is blocked though..."

Good luck. And have fun with your storytelling.

Chapter Thirteen
Work Ethic

The title of this book is *Writing Is Not Work*, and I threw in a chapter called Work Ethic. Seems odd, doesn't it? A wee bit, admittedly, but there's a reason for this.

Writing should never be work. Shouldn't feel like work, look like work, quack like work. Make writing fun, and you'll "work" on your fiction more. This is still my argument, and has been throughout the book.

And to be clear, sometimes you have to be two-faced with the people you live with. Tell them you have to "work on your writing tonight", and they'll respect your time and need for privacy while at the writing chair. When you've shooed all the loved ones out of your office, put on your other face and have fun while making stuff up.

For those of us participating in NaNo (and those writing all year-round, I hope), there's another dimension to this "make writing fun" theme. I'm referring to the process of getting to your office and sitting in the chair.

Work ethic.

By this, I mean dedication and persistence at a task. I wish the English language had another word for work, one that means or implies "work that's fun to do". If such a word exists, I can't think of it readily, and I doubt it's common enough to make sense to most people.

So, work ethic is my best way to express what I mean, unfortunate as that may be. In American culture, "work" and "work ethic" have blue collar connotations: the craftsman who sweats and toils for long hours at a job he does not necessarily enjoy doing.

Try your best to scrub that image out of your brain. Writing can be a job and a career, you can "work" at your fiction, but never turn it into something you dread. Always approach writing with a mental attitude of excitement and joy. Teach and train your mind to see fiction writing as playtime. Might take a long time, maybe even require professional help, but well worth the mental adjustment.

Those who have completed NaNo (wrote 50,000 words in 30 days, or whatever your personal goal was) know that completing the event involves a great deal of dedication and persistence every day, for the entire month. Doing a little bit every day is better than speed typing a lot in one or two days. Few people can complete a novel in five days, so it's better to just keep at it, working at a steady pace.

(A novel in five days is possible, by the way. If you don't believe me, look up an author named Michael Moorcock and search for essays and commentary on how he used Lester Dent's master plot formula.)

The key with completing a novel is to keep at it, no matter how you feel about it on any given day. This is work ethic. Set a goal, stick with it through thick and thin. When you fall off your goal (everybody falls off), you climb back on and try again.

Your mood on any given day will not affect the quality of your words. Hard to believe, I know. But I've written through enough headaches and heartaches to have seen this first hand. I always think what I wrote on my "off-day" was terrible, and the next day looking back I saw no difference in quality. So write when you do feel like it, and when you don't.

Once you've gotten to the writing chair for enough days and diligently written sentence after sentence, you'll have a novel that didn't exist before. The question is, how do you develop a work ethic for a fun activity like writing?

In the chapter Time & Speed, I demonstrated how to make good use of time and "write fast". Use those same lessons to make a daily or weekly goal. Wake up early and write 500 words is a good goal. Set your daily goal to be achievable, but make sure to challenge yourself. If the 500 words in the morning is suddenly feeling too easy, push it to 600.

Keep this in mind: you want to go for an average.

Some days you'll miss. Other days you'll overachieve. Some days you'll be able to hit 5,000 words. Most days might not be so productive. But at the end of the month, if you have 50,000 words total, you'll have averaged 1,667 words per day.

And when you average out your word counts over longer periods—months, or a full year—the days you miss become rounding errors. But only if you get to the writing chair regularly and make the keys go clickety-clack.

The "Rules" of Writing

So, you want to be a writer. What are some habits you need?

First and foremost: **You must write.**

Duh. You're not a writer if you aren't writing. So figure out a schedule that's works for you and the folks you live with. Stick to that schedule. Get used to writing wherever and whenever you can. On the bus. In the airport. At the doctor's office. In the coffee shop. At home in your own office.

Now: **You must finish what you write.**

You can't say you've written a book until you've finished one. Sentence by sentence, scene by scene, bird by bird. Be an artist. Go where the story takes you and finish what you started.

You have the book completed, edited, proofed, and your mother loves it. But now you want to be a published author. What now?

Two more little rules to live by...

You must put the story on the market. Send it to an editor. Not a developmental editor (or a plot doctor, whatever they're called now), but an acquisitions editor at an imprint or a magazine. This is somebody who can pay you money for your story, in return for the rights to publish it.

Or indie publish it. Set up your own imprint as a doing-business-as (DBA). Learn how to make cover art, to format e-books and trade paperbacks, how to be a business person.

Okay, got it. Now what?

You must keep the story on the market. If you submitted the novel to an editor and she rejected it, send it to another editor. Repeat after each rejection, until the novel sells.

Or, if you're an indie publisher, you just keep the book in all the worldwide distribution channels. Don't touch it! Maybe change the cover art every five years, but otherwise just keep it out there and indie pub more books.

Students of science fiction history will recognize I gave a quick synopsis of Robert Heinlein's business rules above. These rules apply to the business of writing as much now as they did in Heinlein's heyday. Writers write and finish what they write. Then they put their stories on the market for others to enjoy. That's the nature of the industry.

Many of you will also notice I skipped a rule in there. Oops. Well, there's a reason I've side-stepped this topic until now, near the end.

Heinlein's infamous rule number three is: **You must refrain from rewriting, except to editorial demand.**

Note, he didn't say (to my knowledge) *never* rewrite. Only *refrain from.*

Perhaps some context will help. Two things about Heinlein...

One, for much (maybe *all*) of his career, Heinlein didn't have a word or text processor. He wrote on a typewriter. That means a rewrite was a literal start from scratch with blank pages. Such an undertaking is time consuming on a typewriter.

Second, until the book distribution collapse of the late 1950's, Heinlein got paid by the word. It was typical in those days for publishing houses and magazines to pay one cent per word, and many pulp writers made fortunes selling stories at that rate. (Many of the most prolific authors in the pulp era wrote upwards of a million words per year, for decades. At one cent per word, that was a lot of money in those days.)

If Heinlein rewrote his stories, he would've had a problem with diminishing returns. Meaning, with every rewrite, he'd get less penny for his bang (okay, bad typewriter pun). He'd have to work twice as long to make one story sale, when without a rewrite he could use the same time to complete two stories.

The number of rewrites you need for any given novel is entirely personal, and subjective. I have my own methods and opinions. I think the problem with diminishing returns is still an issue in our modern age, so my opinion is anything beyond two drafts is redundant and probably unnecessary. (Although I'll say I'm a two- or three-draft writer in public, which is kind of true, if you include the proofing and typo-fixing stage.)

(Word of caution: rewriting is a critical voice activity, unless you've trained yourself to rewrite in creative voice. That's harder than it sounds. There's a reason many otherwise excellent books become dulled when rewritten too much... the author's critical voice destroys everything the creative voice put into the story.)

That said, every writer is different. Some writers need the extra rewrites to fully develop an idea. Others only need one draft. And then there's everything in between. Any path is fine, as long as it's your own and you know the reasons for choosing your path.

The point of this little excursion into Heinlein's rules was to get you to think about your productivity and work ethic. To be a writer, you must write. No other way around it.

Finish every story, publish, start new stories. Have a work ethic when you sit down at the desk.

Trust me, the more you write, the more joy you'll get from your "work". Have fun, write with joy.

Chapter Fourteen
Be a Rebel

A long time ago, back when I walked to school up-hill in the snow both ways, I was taught to write in MLA format. Modern Language Association, for any-one who doesn't know. Along the way I also managed to learn the American Psychological Association (APA) format. Not sure how that happened, must've been in college.

I still have *A Writer's Reference: Fourth Edition* by Diana Hacker, which an English professor made me buy. The front cover boasts that it's updated with both the MLA's and APA's 1999 guidelines.

Do I ever use it? Nope.

How about that copy of *Elements of* Style, by Strunk and White? Nope.

Haven't touched either of those books for years. More than a decade, in the case of *A Writer's Reference*. Grammar, spelling, and standard word usage are all useful for clarity and good writing. Learn the rules of the game... syntax, punctuation, how to form paragraphs, etc.

After these basics are mastered, you can begin to learn how to write stories. By this, I mean plotting, character tags, dialogue, pacing, emotion, sensory depth, setting, and so much more.

After some years have passed, you'll understand you don't really know crap about storytelling. There is simply no ceiling to how much can be learned in our art, and no way to truly master it.

Keep learning. Every day when possible.

So why don't I use my reference books anymore? Partly because I've moved beyond them. Over the course of my life I've had enough practice with punctuation, grammar, and proper usage that I'm comfortable sitting down at a computer and typing one word after another. I make mistakes, sure. But I know how to fix mistakes, too, especially after a trusted first reader points them out.

The other reason is I've learned that good storytelling has nothing to do with pretty words and grammatically correct sentences. The words and rules are just black marks on the page, so we can all agree on what stuff means. Storytelling happens below the surface of the words, in the guts, hearts, and minds of readers.

Storytelling is an act of mind control. You, the writer, control the reader's experiences and emotion as she gets lost in your tale. A very hard skill to learn, for sure. The mind control is done not with word choices; but with skill at building tension, pacing of scenes, point of view depth, and myriad other tools the best authors use.

Perhaps you're still learning the basics of grammar. So what? Write stories anyway. Write many stories, one per day if you can. Call those stories practice sessions, and give them to a trusted reader who will not be overly critical of your work. Keep practicing, keep studying, never stop learning even when you think you've learned it all. You haven't.

The market is full of writing advice books out there. Not hard to find bloggers who are willing to share their knowledge of the craft and the business. Information is easier to get than ever, all without necessarily leaving your home.

Some advice is good, some is outright bad, much of it falls somewhere in between. Perhaps you found my book unhelpful, maybe even dangerous to the process you want to follow. At least you know what not to do, and that's okay.

The difficulty is in deciding who to listen to. I'm afraid I have no useful advice here, except to explore with a mind that is both open and skeptical at the same time. Try out different ways of doing things, much like you'd try on different clothing styles to figure out *your style*.

And that is what voice is. The pesky little thing you can neither see nor hear all too well, but know deep down it's there. Your style of writing and seeing the world, that is your voice. Only you possess it and know how to use it. No one else can exactly imitate it.

To find your voice, you must decide what methods and processes work for you. I've tried to keep my own methods behind a curtain, because I know many of my tricks flat won't work for many people. But in writing a book about *voice*, I've had use my own voice. If I hadn't, this book would've been dull, like a college paper written in MLA format.

You're not writing a novel to please your English professor, so don't use a "standard" format like MLA, APA, Chicago, etc. Just write what's on your mind, in the form of a story told by a character in a setting. Let the character come alive through the black marks on the page and, with enough practice in the craft, your voice will shine through.

Be a rebel. Don't follow the herd or the pack. Don't let others tell you what you should be writing. Never follow market trends or any such silliness. Write to your passions. As Stephen King says, write what scares you.

Much of the advice floating around the NaNo forums doesn't work for me. So you're not supposed to go back and fix things? Right... I write out of order all the time, and I have to cycle backwards in my story to be able to go forwards. I don't even consider my cycling as "editing" or "rewriting", because I'm usually adding new words. Scenery, sensory detail, Chekov's gun, character tags, etc. Adding this stuff in while it's fresh in my head helps me keep the story moving. Adding it later, after the first draft, is just drudgery in my humble opinion.

How about using the Traveling Shovel of Death when I'm stuck? (Note: the TSoD is an ongoing tradition on the NaNo forums. It's a plot device some folks find useful when they're stuck.) I have no problem with killing off characters, which is how the TSoD is normally used, but if I need a laser cannon and a tripwire, I'll pass on the shovel. And again, just more drudgery to edit the damn thing out later.

(Editing bores the crap out of me, if it's not obvious already.)

I could go on, but if you've read this far then you've already seen a little slice of my bag of tricks, which I don't normally share in public. I don't share, because I'm in the minority opinion on many things. You're unlikely to find many people like me on the

NaNo forums or at write-ins, and when you do you won't know it. We're just as happy to keep doing what we do, whether you know about our methods or not.

Like I've said way back at the beginning, take what works and leave the rest. Your mileage **will** vary from mine. Every writer is different, with a unique skill set and a special viewpoint. Use your uniqueness to an advantage.

All of us, in the beginning years of learning the art of fiction, look for rules to follow. Here's a rule all should follow, and never forget: **Be yourself.**

Same advice given when dealing with first date jitters. She'll like you better if you pulled the stick out of your ass and remain calm, even when you're convinced you've made of a fool of yourself. Readers are the same, too.

(Now you know the extent of my dating advice. I won't be writing a book on that topic.)

So be different from all the rest. Be a rebel soul and use your own voice to tell the stories only you can tell.

Chapter Fifteen
Fun

Quite a journey this has been, writing this goofy book. Starting off, I had no idea what it was about other than a few basic themes. *Writing is not work, but fun.* And, *how to find your voice in fiction writing.*

I had figured 30,000 words would be too bloated for such a title, and 10,000 too slim. Turned out a bit under 20,000. My "outline" was little more than a checklist of topics I thought appropriate. I had nineteen listed, four of them didn't make the cut. And two chapters are left unfinished because I got halfway into them and decided they didn't belong.

I wrote entirely out of order, except the introduction was written first and what you're reading now came last. The writing process took me about two weeks, not counting a full week where I dithered on some fiction projects. At the end of it, I think it's fair to say I spent between 20 and 25 hours writing. Tack a few more hours for production time (cover art, formatting, copyedits).

Why go through all that uncertainty, time, and effort? Especially for a book that nobody might read (worst case scenario) or may not appreciate or find useful. What dragged me to the chair, so I could write a chapter every day?

Nothing dragged me.

I went of my own volition.

Because I had fun writing this.

Sure, I had other reasons, too. The big reason that started this project rolling in my head was what happened in the first half of 2015. Or rather, what didn't happen.

I had deep critical voice issues roughly from January to June. Nothing I wrote seemed all that good, or fun, or even original. I had a hard time sitting in the chair for more than ten minutes. I wrote, sure, but my production crept to a standstill. I wondered if maybe the dream was dead and I should pack up and move on to something else.

I took a hard look at everything. My attitude, my fears, my habits. I read books on writing, studied business, and discovered entertaining novels. Finally, in June, I devised a strategy to get past my critical voice and fears.

Every day for a week, I was going to write 250 words in the morning.

The next week, the goal was 400 words or die trying.

Then 500. 750 a day. 1,000. And more.

I got back into the swing of writing, and found out I had missed having the daily habit. Soon, every morning when I woke up, I started looking forward to writing. I was happy achieving my tiny daily goals. And I was accomplishing things, slow at first, and then I picked up momentum.

Now, I'm not paying much attention to the goals I set for myself over a month ago. I'm exceeding my daily word count goal, mostly because I wanted to finish *Writing Is Not Work* before a certain life event comes up around the corner. An event that I foresaw, and planned for. And I hit my deadline, though just barely.

I'm having fun, even when this silly project didn't seem to have an end in sight and I was stumbling around in the darkness. Writing this book helped clarify in my head what I was going through. And wow, did I learn much in this process. Stuff about myself, about my methods, my philosophies, and how to be a better writer.

But I have another reason for writing this book. Last November, I had some serious disillusionment with NaNo. The way people talk both on the forums and at write-ins. The advice that gets passed around. The methods people employ to finish 50,000 words in 30 days.

None of that truly represented me as a writer and artist. I march to my own drum, with methods that work for me and might not be suitable for the vast majority of writers.

Where was my clan?

I've had the pleasure of interacting with and being mentored by good people who use the tools I've outlined here. But none of those folks I met through NaNo. Not many young writers understand Heinlein's business rules on a deep level (whether you follow them or not is irrelevant... you can still understand them). Not many wrimos, I'm afraid, understand what it means to craft a story with your unique voice.

So I wrote this book for all you weirdos and hell-raisers, who don't entirely climb into the box and follow "da rulez". *Writing Is Not Work* won't help everyone, but I hope it helps out those who need to see a different perspective than what's commonly offered every November.

Writing was not fun for me for quite awhile. Now it is, since I've been working on things to develop my voice and craft. The learning never stops, and there's no ceiling to bump your head on.

The final piece of learning in how to find and use your voice is *the doing*. You must write, and finish your stories. Then write more stories, and keep learning.

I can explain to you the mechanics of playing Space Invaders on the Atari console. Really not much to it. The game controller had a stick and two red buttons. You moved your guy on the horizontal axis. Shoot the aliens before they land.

But to deeply understand Space Invaders, you have to play it. Attaining the high scores in that game is stupidly hard. Knowing when to fire, when to ignore the aliens and shoot the mothership, how to use cover while you have it. So many details. So hard to do. Which is what made the game addicting.

Writing is no different than a game, when you get down to it. Frustrating at times, impossible to truly master, addicting when you find your mojo.

And now I'm off to other projects. What happens after that? I don't know. Don't want to know. I follow the siren's call that whispers impure thoughts in my head.

Go. Do. Write!

I hope you approach your novels with a sense of wonder and excitement. Have fun and don't give up the dream.

I wish you well in all your endeavors.

Recommended Reading

These are some books I've found useful. Maybe they will help you, too.

Kevin J. Anderson. *Million Dollar Productivity.*
Leah Cutter. *Business for Breakfast, Volume 1: The Beginning Professional Writer.*
Jerrold Mundis. *Break Writer's Block Now!*
Laura Resnick. *Rejection, Romance, and Royalties: The Wacky World of a Working Writer.*
Kristine Kathryn Rusch. *The Pursuit of Perfection: And How It Harms Writers.*
Kristine Kathryn Rusch. *The Write Attitude.*
Dean Wesley Smith. *Killing the Top Ten Sacred Cows of Publishing.*
Dean Wesley Smith. *Writing Into the Dark.*
Douglas Smith. *Playing the Short Game: How to Market & Sell Short Fiction.*

About the Author

D. Anthony Brown is a writer in Minnesota. He's been to school a few times, but now days he mostly teaches himself new things; such as how to play the guitar, Tarot, and whatever topics interest him at any given moment. He is an avid reader and an addicted gamer.

On the National Novel Writing Month website, he goes by the highly unoriginal handle dabrownofmn. He may also be contacted at danthonybrown.com.

Want more stories from D. Anthony Brown? Sign up for the newsletter on his website and receive word about new and upcoming titles!

Thank you for purchasing this book!

You may also have a copy on your favorite e-reading device, free of charge. To do so, follow these steps:

1. Create an account at Smashwords (or login if you already have an account there).
2. Search for this book (*Writing Is Not Work* by D. Anthony Brown).
3. Use the following coupon code at checkout: **XW92Z**

The code will give you a 100% discount on this title and lasts for five years from the publication of this title. The following formats are available:

MOBI, EPUB, PDF, RTF, LRF, PDB, HTML, and plain text

Note: the code is good for five years from original publication date. If the code doesn't work, contact the publisher at:
david (at) d anthony brown (dot) com